Mark Wheeller

Too Much Punch for Judy

2020 revised edition

Salamander Street

PLAYS

Too Much Punch for Judy was first published by the Institute of Alcohol Studies, 1988 (ISBN 1871195004)

Too Much Punch for Judy was published by Dbda in 1999; Reprinted in July 2002, November 2003, March 2005, July 2006 & September 2016. (ISBN 9781902843056)

This edition first published in 2020 by Salamander Street Ltd., 87 Ivor Court, Gloucester Place, London NW1 6BP (info@salamanderstreet.com)

Too Much Punch for Judy © Mark Wheeller, 1987, 1999-2006

PB ISBN: 9781913630300
E ISBN: 9781913630317

Cover and text design by Konstantinos Vasdekis

Printed and bound in Great Britain

10 9 8 7 6 5 4 3 2 1

Further copies of this publication can be purchased from www.salamanderstreet.com

CONTENTS

Acknowledgements

Sources: "Judy" and her family; PC Abrahams; PC Caten; Essex County Council Highways Department; Essex Police; Sister Hunt; "Duncan" and The West Essex Gazette.

All the sources for kind permission to use their words.

The performers in the Epping Youth Theatre productions *Quenchers* (1986) and *Too Much Punch for Judy* (1987): Kim Baker; Fay Davies; Jo Dumelow; Paul Elliott; Nick Fradd; Ryan Gilbey; George Griffiths; Emma Jefferson; Garth Jennings; Debbie Mitchell; Debbie Pollard; Jo Redman; John Rowley; Barrie Sapsford; Beth Spendlow; Emma Turner; Anna Wallbank and John Ward.

Mick and Sylvia Baker for their initial inspiration and their tremendous support throughout the EYT performances.

CADD (Campaign Against Drinking and Driving) for their tremendous campaign.

Derek Rutherford, Institute of Alcohol Studies.

Rosie Walsh & David Lyndsay (then of Essex County Council Highways Department) for their support.

Frank Nunneley (then of Hertfordshire County Council – Road Safety) and all the Road Safety Officers in England, Scotland and Wales who have offered their support to the play's continued success.

Ken Boyden for taking the play to New Zealand for such successful tours.

Mat Kane, Antony Audenshaw and Yvonne Allen, and the Ape Theatre Company for their stunning performances since 1988 in England, Cyprus, Germany, Jersey.

To Mat, Steve, Fay, and Tor (Ape Theatre Company) for inspiring the opening and closing scenes.

Alistair Black, Hampshire County Council Drama Inspector, for the idea to revisit the beginning of the play at the end nice one!

Sophie Gorell Barnes and all at MBA Literary Agency for continued belief and support.

Dbda for publishing this play when other publishers had turned it down so often!

Thanks to George Spender and those in the Salamander Street team for their efforts to extend the reach of my plays.

Rachel Wheeller and family.

Introduction to the 2020 edition

No one is more surprised than me at the enormous success achieved (so quickly) by *Too Much Punch for Judy*, which I wrote initially as a twenty-minute end section to a Youth Theatre play, *Quenchers*, about alcohol abuse. Since those initial performances in 1987 until 2018, *Too Much Punch for Judy* has toured non-stop throughout schools, colleges, prisons, young offenders institutes and army bases. It has also been performed extensively in Australia, Cyprus, N. Ireland, Éire, Germany, New Zealand, Norway, the USA (Texas), Spain, Canada, Singapore, South Africa, Hong Kong, Dubai and Vietnam.

In 1991, I was awarded the Prince Michael of Kent Special Award for Services to Road Safety Education for the play. *Too Much Punch for Judy* is now one of the most (if not the most) performed contemporary plays, with 6058 licensed performances between 1987 and 2020... all this from a twenty-minute "extra" at the end of a production about alcohol misuse.

By the Christmas of 1985 the outline structure of our Youth Theatre play dealing with the dangers of alcohol was, we thought, complete. Then I saw the emotive (and very effective) Christmas drink/drive campaign. The subject of drinking and driving had not even crossed my mind... times were very different then. Drink/driving was something that everyone knew happened but few really thought seriously about it. Here was a real challenge for the play; to flag up a really important issue and encourage an awareness of what was evidently a massive problem.

Shortly after, I spoke to our Schools Police Liaison Officer who put me in contact with PC Chris Caten who, in turn, introduced me to "Judy".

> **JUDY:** *Chris Caten explained that there was a local playwright looking for a story about drinking and driving. He wasn't at all sure that I'd want to do it but, as he knew me quite well thought it was worth sounding me out. I thought... well... alright then, if someone's that interested I will... especially as Chris thought it was such a good idea. I didn't view the details of the accident as private, I'd dropped a bollock and, well, it didn't matter to me how many people knew, so long as it was going to do some good somewhere along the line.*

The local paper, the *West Essex Gazette* (who were always so supportive of the play), had been particularly sensitive in their coverage at the time of the accident, writing no more than a brief report. Consequently, the incident had not been "big" local news so, few people actually knew Judy's story. There were even details of it, the research for this play uncovered, that Judy herself didn't know... she was, for example, completely unaware that anyone arrived on the scene prior to Chris Caten.

I met Judy on the 3rd January 1986. She was a wonderful subject to interview; she was incredibly open, making it easy for me to ask probing questions and, in describing events, quite naturally quoted lines of dialogue. I admired (and still do) her courage in coming forward. I left her house that day with the play planned out clearly in my head. It fell into place very naturally from that point on.

> **JUDY:** *The main thing I remember about that first interview was getting upset at the point where I remembered I said 'Oh no… not my beautiful sister'. I remember having to stop at that point thinking I was going to start crying and feeling really stupid.*

From initial interviews I conducted with Judy, her mum, Chris Caten, PC Abrahams, "Duncan" and Sister Davis, I was able to jigsaw together the first draft of the play.

I set myself the challenge of only using words spoken in the interviews to ensure that the play "rang true"… as true as joint memories would allow. Consequently, the first draft was dense with monologues but it gave me a starting point to return to the relevant interviewees, to tease out more dialogue and check what had been selected for authenticity.

Finally Judy, Vi, Chris and myself had a meeting and went through each of the scenes where two or more of them appeared together. This was amazing. It ironed out any inconsistencies and also inspired new memories and therefore new words for the script.

> **JUDY:** *If you're going to do an autobiographical play like this I think it's best to use the person's words to capture the way they speak, otherwise you can't begin to understand what sort of person they are. This wasn't a fairy tale to be messed around with… it's something that actually happened and, anyway, I don't think it would have had half the impact.*

One rehearsal, just a week before the premiere of *Quenchers*, illustrates how close this method of writing had come to getting the script 'right'.

We were having difficulty staging the section where Chris reveals to Judy that her sister had been killed. The words were fine but we couldn't figure out how we should stage Chris. Should he be standing, kneeling beside her how close should he be? I asked Chris to come in and add his comments. Chris watched but his suggestions didn't seem to work. Then I asked Chris to do the scene but of course he didn't know the words.

"No problem!" I retorted, "Just improvise."

Chris improvised and our Judy (Kim Baker) at that time, said the words from the script. Chris was able to show us how he broke the news and, with few exceptions he used the words we had in our script. For the record he knelt beside her and held her hand. I remember some time afterwards the police said they used this scene as an example of recommended police behaviour in this kind of situation.

Many who have seen the play say how powerful this approach was (it is now often referred to as Verbatim Theatre – this was written before that description was coined) and comment on the authenticity of the words. The success and effectiveness of *Too Much Punch for Judy* stems from the fact that it is true and "Judy" is real.

No attempt should be made in presenting the play to hide this fact, indeed by the use of slides of the real incident, the "reality" can be highlighted to the audience. This Brechtian approach was the one used by the Epping Youth Theatre when they presented the first version of the play as the end piece to *Quenchers* with the real Judy in the audience for the first time. It proved hugely successful.

> **JUDY:** *I breezed through getting ready. I breezed into Harlow Playhouse, got into the theatre and nearly lost control. I was flinching all the time and it made me sweat trying not to lose control. I didn't know whether to cry and walk out or be sick and walk out. I remember there were some young blokes, they were about eighteen, across from us, and they were crying. I was surprised. I never thought it would genuinely upset people like that, I really didn't.*

Throughout the (long) run of *Quenchers* we picked up some tremendous reviews and also gained the interest and support of the Essex County Council Road Safety Department. A very fruitful relationship quickly developed and they sponsored our performances at the Edinburgh Fringe Festival. Everyone thought this would be a fitting end to this hugely successful project. I had other ideas. It was only the beginning!

I could see that the final section of *Quenchers* (sub-titled *Too Much Punch for Judy*, after a little-known national Christmas drink/drive campaign) had enormous potential, as yet unrealised but it had only told half the story. I began to realise that, rather than the night of the fatal accident appearing on its own, out of context, I should tell the story of Joanna and Judy from childhood. Fortunately, Judy was more than willing to co-operate, so I organised an interview which, like the others before, would be taped and painstakingly transcribed by hand.

Judy talked openly about her childhood years and her relationship with Jo giving me plenty of material to work with. I combined these interviews with what her mother had said in her original interview and jigsawed together a new opening section telling of Judy's early years and made a number of developments to the accident section.

Too Much Punch for Judy received its first public performance on Thursday 12th February 1987 in front of about forty people in the small drama studio at St. Johns School, Epping.

> **JUDY:** *I thought that it was better than the extract in Quenchers. I thought it had more effect. It's not something I can enjoy. I switch off emotionally, otherwise I'd cry. When you're not ready for it, it does give you a bit of a wallop.*

The reviews following this performance were universally excellent.

Soon, Essex County Council were telling me that they wanted to sponsor a tour of the play. They would pay for the play to be performed in every school in Essex. I couldn't believe it! Unfortunately, it was unrealistic to release the Youth Theatre from their studies for eight weeks, so as second choice, a professional TIE company were hired (Touchstone Theatre In Education Company) and the tour, much to my surprise, happened. The next thing I knew was that someone from Scotland had seen the play and they wanted it to tour Scottish schools. Since then it has toured across Britain (Ape Theatre Company) every year up until 2014 when government cutbacks led to the road safety departments who funded it being disbanded.

The next invitation was for the play to tour throughout Éire... then New Zealand. I was even invited out (paid for by the British Council... thanks!) to see the play and lead some workshops. Amazing! It became the most performed play in New Zealand with John Godber's *Bouncers* coming in second!

It was subsequently performed by the critically acclaimed TESTO in Norway and Michelle Smith's (one of the founder members of Paper Birds) Love Theatre in Jersey.

Throughout this time, school/college drama departments began to put on their own productions of the play. The ones that I have seen have been outstanding. It has won numerous One Act Play Festival awards.

When I was an examiner for GCSE Drama I often read students' glowing reviews of Ape's performances. More recently I have been approached for permission to use extracts for A-Level or audition speeches and to that end, I have adapted a monologue which will, I hope, prove useful to such students. All this from the smallest of small plays! It seemed that nothing could go wrong. But it did.

Late in the evening, shortly after the 5th October 1993, I received a phone call from Chris Caten. His tone immediately told me that something dreadful had happened. Nothing could prepare me for what he was about to say; Judy had been involved in a second drink/drive incident. Her car had collided with another and killed the twenty-one-year-old driver (Penny Jessup) immediately.

This tragedy defied belief. The emotional consequences for all involved, were more far reaching than I could ever imagine. The awful events (included in this version of the play with a fuller context than in any previous version) speak for themselves. A road safety officer shocked me further by saying that, sadly, this incident supported statistics: Once you have been convicted of drinking and driving... you are more likely, statistically, to offend again than someone who has never done so! Do people never learn? That has led me to pose the question to frame this version of the play...

If Judy didn't learn from being involved in the incident, can we honestly expect people in an audience watching this play to allow their behaviour to be affected?

Despite this, I remain convinced that it can be a potent message for many. But of course I would say that, I guess. It's certainly an interesting debate.

I sincerely hope that in continuing to promote this play we can all do our best to raise the issues and ensure that there are fewer tragedies around the corner.

It is estimated that *Too Much Punch for Judy* has been seen by nearly a million young people over the last thirty or so years. The powerful tool of live theatre has been well served by the many versions of the play and the message of 'safe driving practices' communicated effectively and imaginatively by many theatre groups. How many lives have been saved? No one can answer that. Originally the aim of this play was to help put the problem of drinking and driving 'on the agenda'. I am certain that it has gone way beyond that.

It has also, I hope, made drama lessons more enticing and exciting. I love visiting schools often delivering workshops on animating monologues and, of course, the accident scene. When I first heard this story I knew that had to be the centrepiece of the play. We had to stage it. Neither I nor my Youth Theatre members had any model on which to base how we should do it. There was no Frantic Assembly... no physical theatre groups that we were aware of. We didn't let this put us off. To tell this story we had to stage this scene... and so we did, progressively well as time went on. The version you can see in the OYT 25th Anniversary production is to date (2020) the definitive presentation of this scene. I am very proud to say it was directed by my son Charlie, who wasn't even born when the play was written. He is now a circus performer (Barely Methodical Troupe) and my instruction to him before I left him with my cast was 'bring a bit of circus to it'. And he did! Thanks, Charlie.

I have also loved writing a resource book which has been published by Salamander Street alongside this script. This was designed by Barrie Sapsford who was in the very first production of this play when it was a twenty minute add-on to our *Quenchers* play. It was very much a labour of love developed on the request of teachers and students who wanted to know more about the play. This volume tells you everything you could ever want to know. It's not that I have a great memory (I don't) but I kept production diaries at the time, which with all this interest in the play have proved unexpectedly useful!

This is a genuinely 'new' publication. It includes all the updates I made in the previous one where I went through all the interviews and spotted parts that I missed first time round. I also made small alterations to the order of the 'jig-saw' and have consciously made a point of stressing certain moments that had been previously passed over. I also discovered for this edition an interview transcription I did with Judy after the second incident. There was some of this I'd not included previously but now I think the time is right to reveal it. I have also included some of the context for that second incident. I had always been fearful that to do so would be seen to be offering a justification of what happened. I don't intend it to be that, and nor would Toni. It is merely the facts that led to the situation she found herself in. It is my decision to include these words in this publication. I hope it adds to our understanding of an appalling situation for anyone to be in.

I hope that the increased availability of this play script will lead to new performances in new territories and new audiences so that the openly propagandist message is spelt out to even more people young and old alike.

Don't drink and drive.

Props and Presentation

This play should be presented simply, yet imaginatively.

Few props are required:

A wheelchair, two sets of car keys and two half-filled beer glasses.

Be imaginative with the other props... They can be much more symbolic: empty beer crates (to sit on), a sheet (for the decorating scene / baby Leanne) and scaffolding poles for the accident scene.

Too Much Punch for Judy received its professional premiere by Touchstone Theatre In Education Company in May 1987.

Characters

6 male, 6 female, 1 male or female.

JUDY
A woman in her early twenties

VI
Judy's mother

JO
Judy's sister

PETE
Judy's husband (*a non speaking part*)

BOB
A cocky 'lad'

NOB
Bob's sidekick

VOICES/ACTORS
Male or female

DUNCAN
The first person on the scene of the accident

P.C. CATEN
Local Police Constable, friend of Judy's family

P.C. ABRAHAMS
Fresh, 'out of the box' Police Constable

SISTER/CHARGE NURSE DAVIS
Responsible for Judy in Hospital, male or female

NARRATORS 1 & 2
Male or female

ACTOR 1
FEMALE

MARK
Playwright (sixties)

RON
Penny Jessup's father (fifties)

SIMON SPENCE
Author

With doubling this play can be presented by
2 male, 2 female with parts allocated as follows:

FEMALE 1
Judy

FEMALE 2
Ron, Narrator 2, Vi, Jo,

MALE 1
Bob, Voice, P.C. Caten (taking P.C. Abrahams' lines), Narrator 1

MALE 2
Mark, Nob, Pete, Voice, Duncan, Charge Nurse Davis

Prologue

Written for the 2020 Version

JUDY *sits centrally on the stage with* **JO** *immediately on her left, as though in the same car in the passenger seat. They are surrounded by people armed with scaffolding poles ready to attack them.* **CHRIS** *is on stage in full police costume observing, opposite* **MARK**.

Accompanied by loud shouts, and a single swing of the scaffolding bars towards **JO**, *the following lines are shrieked simultaneously.*

ALL: Judy, slow down a bit! **JUDY:** Aaaaargh!

JUDY *remains untouched by the poles.* **JO** *is hurled back.*

Silence.

ACTOR 1: Between 1985 and 1987 Mark Wheeller *(Indicates.)* wrote *Too Much Punch for Judy.*

MARK: Judy felt this could be a way of bringing some good from her tragedy.

ACTOR 1: Judy had killed her sister, Jo, *(***JO** *exits slowly.)* in a drink drive incident in North Weald, where she lived. *(***ACTOR 1** *takes up a position in front of* **JUDY***'s seat.)*

MARK: PC Chris Caten *(Indicates.)* organised interviews for me. All the words in the script are from those interviews as spoken by the people involved.

ACTOR 1: The play became a key part of international drink drive campaigns.

MARK: Then, in 1993, *(Pace slows.)* the unbelievable happened.

A simple representation of a car accident is repeated again accompanied by loud shouts of the following lines spoken simultaneously together with the single swing of scaffolding bars, this time felling **ACTOR 1**.

ALL: Judy, slow down a bit! **JUDY:** Aaaaargh!

Silence.

MARK: Judy was driving along the same stretch of road where she had crashed and Jo had been killed, ten years earlier.

200 metres from that location, Judy's car, on the wrong side of the road, hit another car killing the twenty-one-year-old driver, Penny Jessup.

Once again, Judy had been drinking. She was twice over the legal limit and had traces of cannabis in her blood.

Chris Caten phoned to inform me late that evening. I couldn't believe what I was hearing.

(MARK and PC CATEN are on the phone.)

PC CATEN: Oh and another thing, Mark. The press will want a quote. You should prepare something.

MARK: Okay. I shall. Thanks, Chris.

(They put down their phones. PC CATEN exits.)

The final line of *Too Much Punch* was echoing in my head:

JUDY: I will never drink and drive again as long as I live... never ever... I just couldn't do it.

MARK: I am a very black and white kind of a person so, I thought talking to Judy would imply my support lay exclusively with her, when my sympathies actually lay with twenty-one-year-old Penny and her family. However, the situation regarding the future of the play demanded that I meet with Judy *(MARK heads towards the area of the stage that will, for the next few moments, become JUDY's house.)* and... I came to understand something my wife often said to me:

Mark, not every situation is black and white.

MARK: *(Arriving and seeing JUDY as she opens her front door.)* When Judy answered the door she started to cry. This was no moment to be judgemental and I spontaneously gave her a hug. She took me inside and we soon started talking. I was reminded of how 'ballsy' she had been in those original interviews. I remember something she said, which I hadn't used in the play but, *(with a smile.)* it had always stuck in my mind...

JUDY: I don't view the details of the accident as private, I'd dropped a bollock and the world's entitled to know. It really doesn't matter to me how many people know as long as it does some good somewhere along the line.

MARK: Forthright and straight forward... oh and by the way it was me who suggested I alter her name to fit the title... not her. She had been very easy to talk to.

The most harrowing moment was when she revealed her reaction to Chris telling her of Jo's death...

JUDY: Not my sister... not my beautiful sister.

MARK: I remember her voice cracking and she kind of broke down. I offered to stop the interviews but she said:

JUDY: No, it's okay. Just let me get a cup of tea and then we'll carry on.

MARK: This was our first meeting and we were talking about this...

JUDY: I'd never talked about the accident before... not even to my mum.

MARK: The relationship between playwright and subject is unique. From the first moment we met, my sole purpose was to ask her questions... probing questions to be able to tell her story. I wasn't trained to do this... I just did it instinctively. I'd had no time to prepare but now, after all these years we actually did have a relationship... a relationship based on having done this play together, but it was a relationship. My reason for being here was to establish if, following this second incident, she was happy for the play to continue...

JUDY: Of course I am. No question.

MARK: And then, as we relaxed, she let me know she wanted to say something that I might want to put in the play.

I didn't bring anything with me to...

... so straightaway, she offered me some notepaper and a pen, it literally hadn't crossed my mind to do an interview in these circumstances... but... and as she talked, I did ask a few questions.

JUDY: I had nothing to live for after Steve died.

MARK: Judy's husband, Steve Marriott, was a famous super-famous lead singer of the Small Faces and Humble Pie. His career was on a downhill slope but there were signs of a resurgence, as he was in the days prior to his death, recording with Peter Frampton.

JUDY: The world I lived and mixed in is frowned upon.

MARK: She and Steve were getting together in the early days of the play going out on tour. I remember being quite excited if Steve answered the phone. Sometimes he'd indulge me and talk about the play. *(Laughs.)*

I moved away from Epping at this time and our contact lessened to, basically, Christmas card exchanges.

Then, on 21st April 1991, four years after I'd written *Too Much Punch for Judy*, I heard on the news, Steve had been killed in a house fire. I later discovered in his biography that his blood contained quantities of valium, alcohol and cocaine. Judy and his final moments together were spent arguing.

JUDY: It wasn't a normal relationship we had, nor a normal life so I didn't deal with his death like a normal person. I didn't have any interest in my own life. Steve was my life. I slipped into a pattern of drinking... you don't notice... it's like a cup of coffee.

People see drink problems as a falling-down drunk but you can live a completely normally life.

I haven't coped with problems in my life. Drink numbed the pain, helped it to go away but it also led to this.

I've gone into counselling voluntarily. I know I must replace drink with something else in my life. I mean... what have I done to deserve the horrible things that have happened to me?

MARK: Then, referring to Penny, the young woman she'd killed in the second crash...

JUDY: She had everything and she's gone. I have nothing and I'm still here. You'll have to ask God why that is?

I can never pay for what I've done. At least if I go to prison I will have been punished. I must pay some sort of price. People need to feel I've been punished and her parents will want me put away for a long time.

MARK: She broached the subject of saying sorry to Penny's parents before the court case and said how she feared that it may appear like she was doing it to affect the sentence... I wasn't able to scribe this but I remember her saying it.

JUDY: Someone said I should write to her parents to say that I'm sorry. I'm not sure that will help. It goes beyond that doesn't it?

MARK: There were no easy answers. *(MARK gets up to leave.)* We said our goodbyes and as I was about to leave Judy talked about driving to her counselling sessions.

You're allowed to?

JUDY: It's all legal.

MARK: The ban only took effect after she was sentenced... and she was sentenced to five years in prison.

Penny's parents were desolate:

RON JESSUP: I would have liked her to be put in prison and the key thrown away, but I accept that is not reasonable. She has stolen fifty or sixty years of Penny's life and given us a life sentence. We will never, ever forget what she has done.

JUDY: People who know me are upset for me... for what I've got to go through. You can't tell them not to care for me.

MARK: Judy was sent to Holloway Prison and once there, her counselling was curtailed against her wishes. Strange. As a captive audience in prison you'd think it would be best for everyone that it should continue... but that's not how it was. Madness.

JUDY: The second part of my life must be better than the fist part.

MARK: Sadly, that wasn't to be.

In 2020, I had another shocking phone call from Simon Spence. Simon was in the process of writing an oral history biography about Steve (Marriott). He wanted an input from me, about Judy, which I gave him. Just as we were signing off he asked me a question:

SIMON: The day before Steve's death when they'd left America in a hurry and he abandoned a lucrative recording contract, do you know why they left?

MARK: No. All I know is they were arguing all the way home.

SIMON: Yeh.

MARK: Do you know why?

SIMON: Well, it's unconfirmed but...

MARK: ... and he went on to tell me what later appeared in the book, *All or nothing*.

SIMON: I've been told she got a DUI...

MARK: ... driving under the influence...

SIMON: ... and she was so worried about it, given what she'd done before... and being in the USA... so she said to Steve: "Let's get a plane." And they did... they grabbed everything and went straight to the airport.

MARK: I couldn't believe what I was hearing.

I've since read Steve's book and it says she had a serious fall recently. That resulted in a brain haemorrhage. Apparently Judy can no longer speak properly.

Following our meeting to discuss the future of the play I had no further direct contact with Judy. That's sad. I feel a deep sense of loyalty to her, despite what has happened. This play was seismic for me and opened all sorts of doors.

I've often wondered how she was and what had happened to her. I wanted her to've been more settled and... yes... happy. I'd like to've stayed in full contact with her as I do with other people whose stories I tell. I considered her a friend but I also realise, I must represent one part of her life she'd rather forget.

This whole situation has made me reflect on the power of this sort of didactic play... like... am I kidding myself? If Judy couldn't learn from her own mistake, how can I expect a play about it to have an effect on anyone merely watching?

It might seem strange to say this but, I remain convinced it can... and I'm not the only one.

Another thing people ask me is... how do you trust what Judy says? I still believe she was always supremely honest. I am aware now she didn't tell me everything but, what she did tell was raw and brave. No one forced her to do it. She willingly agreed to talk with her mum and me record it, when they'd never discussd the original accident in any detail previously.

At my suggestion, she also agreed to meet with PC Chris Caten to help me to get the scene where her sister's death is revealed to her as accurate as their memories together in the same room would allow. All this to make my play more... authentic. She stood to gain nothing from it. She wanted it to be right... to be helpful to me.

So, while some things may not have been said... what was said was, in my view, raw and not self-censored.

My play continues to be worthwhile and truthful... but don't just believe me... judge for yourselves... watch it... and now you can in full knowledgee of everything that happened afterwards.

So... here it is... *Too Much Punch for Judy*... pretty much as it was when I first put it together back in 1987.

Section 1

OUT ON THE PISS!

25th Anniversary Production

ALL: January 1983:

NARRATOR 1: Breakfast TV arrives in the UK.

*(Loud vocal engine noises as **JUDY** pushes **JO** onto the stage in a wheelchair, very fast, as though they are messing around in a shopping trolley late at night.)*

JO: *(Screaming.)* Judy! Judy! Slow down a bit!

BOB & NOB: Crash!

*(**JO** is tipped off the wheelchair, screaming, she falls to the floor on her back. The action freezes.)*

BOB: Jo and Judy... sisters, out on the town.

NOB: ...with a shopping trolley from the local supermarket.

JUDY: *(Back to life, laughing hysterically.)* Jo? Jo?

JO: My back... Judy... my back.

JUDY: What about your back? You're always on your back!!!

JO: Cheeky tart! Something in my back's clicked.

JUDY: You're having me on?

JO: Course I am!

JUDY: Bloody idiot! *(They laugh. **JO** gets up.)*

JO: Come on... or we'll be late for...

JUDY & JO: Aerobics...

ALL: February 1983.

NARRATOR 1: Playwright Tennessee Williams dies in New York...

NARRATOR 2: ... when he accidently swallows

ALL: ... a plastic bottle cap!

JUDY: At the gym.

JO: Losing weight...

JUDY: Till half past eight...

JO & JUDY: Then... off to the wine bar!

ALL: March 1983.

NARRATOR 1: CDs go on sale in the UK...

NARRATOR 2: Sixteen different albums from CBS records.

JUDY: *(Adopting the voice of typical cookery TV personality.)* Today's new easy to follow recipe is "Smashed out of our Skulls" by Judy...

JO: ... and Jo

JO & JUDY: Ingredients.

JO: Puerile conversation.

JUDY: Wine.

JO: Laughter.

JUDY: More wine!

JO: Visit the loo.

JUDY: And finally...

ALL: More wine!

JUDY: Note:

JO: This recipe can be improved with a healthy portion of...

JO & JUDY: Testosterone!

JO, JUDY, BOB & NOB: Cue... blokes in the wine bar!

ALL: April 1983.

NARRATOR 1: The one pound coin is introduced in England and Wales.

BOB: Bob...

NOB: Nob!

BOB: Looking good...

NOB: ...with slicked back hair.

BOB: Feeling cool...

BOB & NOB: No underwear!

BOB: With throbbing – can't get enough of it – body tone.

NOB: That's why they call us...

BOB & NOB: "Testosterone"

BOB: We are on the look out!

NOB: Fishing line and hook out!

BOB: Watering the nookey drought!

BOB & NOB: Essex girls!!!

JO & JUDY: Like two warriors they approach us...

JO: ...that one's mine!

JUDY: "Good luck to you", I reply, as they trot out...

JO & JUDY: ...their crappy chat up line.

BOB: Look at you two...

BOB & NOB: ...with your curves...

NOB: ...and us...

BOB & NOB: ...us with no brakes.

JO: Judy. What do you think?

JUDY: I think they're...

JO & JUDY: ...plonkers! *(They laugh hysterically.)*

BOB & NOB: Do you wanna drink?

JUDY & JO: *(Dead serious.)* Dry white wine... a bottle... each!

ALL: May 1983:

NARRATOR: Thatcher wins a landslide General Election.

ALL 4: Drink!

BOB: Drink!

JUDY: Drink!

NOB: Drink!

JO: Drink!

(General merriment… perhaps a rowdy [rugby?] song.)

(The pace slows.)

NARRATOR 1: May 20th 1983:

NARRATOR 2: A Friday.

NARRATOR 1: The discovery of the retrovirus that causes AIDS is reported.

JUDY: Part two of our evening…

BOB: A complete change of gear…

NOB: Their good time drink…

JO: Calls death… to appear.

VI: And… in Epping…

JO: Jo…

JUDY: …and Judy

JO & JUDY: …drive home…

VI: Only eight miles to Ongar…

(The pace returns to that of **JUDY** *and* **JO***'s lively night out.)*

JO: A bottle of wine and I'm still standing! *(Laughter.)* Come on Judy, we'd better get out before we're thrown out.

JUDY: Wouldn't it be better if I drove?

JO: No; it's my car, it's my responsibility.

ALL: *(Looking at* **JO***.)* Ignorance!

JUDY: I haven't had as much to drink as you. I'll only be a little over the limit.

ALL: *(Looking at* **JUDY***.)* Ignorance!

JO: Okay then. *(She throws her car keys to* **JUDY***, who catches them.)* You drive.

(Silence.)

The mood changes suddenly. **JUDY** *remains motionless, looking at the keys.*

JO exits as **JUDY** *turns slowly… very slowly… to face the audience. The following lines are said with the obvious pain of the memory.*

JUDY: It was just another night on the piss... but it wasn't... if anyone questioned it, everyone would just say...

BOB: Them two?

NOB: Don't worry about them.

BOB & NOB: They're always pissed!

JUDY: You get so sure of yourself, so clever, well, not clever, you just don't think, 'cos you do it all the time.

It only takes one person to point it out to you and you might not do it. Imagine if I see two people, drunk, who are going to drive home and I went over and told them what had happened to me last time I did it... they'd get a cab wouldn't they?

Section 2

CHILDHOOD AND YOUTH IN RETROSPECT

JUDY: The accident happened on the 20th May 1983. Resigned...
I think that's the word. I'm resigned to the fact that it has happened.
If you go through life with a big guilt complex afterwards, you
just end up hurting everybody else as well as yourself, 'cos you get
bitter and wound up. Nothing I can do is going to change it, ever. I
wouldn't have harmed my sister, Joanna, not on purpose, so I don't
feel guilty about killing her... because it was... an accident. I just
know that I'll never be so out of control that I would put someone
else's life in danger and I have never driven after drinking since.
Before it happens you think... "Oh, I won't get caught." I would
probably never have got stopped and breathalysed. I'm having to pay
for my mistake in a different way.

VI: Tell you a bit about Joanna? *(Sigh.)*
She was very extrovert, full of life, emotional... highly emotional,
but a character. I mean, obviously to me she was beautiful, all your
children are aren't they... but Jo was different. We were really good
friends as well as mother and daughter. Even through my marriage
break up Jo was very strong for me. Judy and Johnnie were both
younger so it was always "Joey and the babies". It's so difficult to
describe her... always willing, kind and thoughtful... an exceptional
person.

JUDY: Joanna was like my Mum's idol.

When I was young I felt a bit left out. I used to run away from
home... to my Nan's... and take my hamster with me. She lived about
a mile away, so I used to walk up there with my little hamster. I used
to ask her not to let Mum know as she'd worry, but my Nan always
rang her up.

VI: To describe Jo or to put her into words is impossible. You had to
know her... well she was just different. I don't think anyone ever said
a bad word about her. Everyone said... "Oh, ain't your Jo a lovely
girl!"

JUDY: I was a bit of a bully, generally threatening people and
frightening them, making them give me money and things, just

horrible, really horrible. I didn't learn nothing at school. I liked English and Drama and got slung out of nearly all my others. My CSE cookery exam... that was a bit of a laugh. You have to make this meal, you know, starter, main course and afters. The starter: I can't remember what happened to that but the main course was spaghetti Bolognese... well, in my case, just Bolognese 'cos I forgot to bring the spaghetti in!

For afters we had to make an apple pie. Mine sunk into the apple and, as if that wasn't bad enough, it then caught fire! You had to put it all on a table with your name on and everything. When the examiner came round she looked at mine and went (*Feigning 'posh' voice.*) "Oh, deary, deary me! Just look at that one! Not very appetising, wouldn't you say?" and then she laughed!... Right out of order. So, I went up to her face, and I says: "Oy that's mine... and do you know what? I couldn't give a toss how 'appetising' you think it is 'cos I don't want to be a chef or nothing... you stupid old tart!" And I walked out saying... "I ain't fucking coming back to this dump no more!" And I didn't. I wasn't that bothered because I had a job at the hairdressers. A while later I got a letter saying to return any books I had that belonged to the school. *(She laughs.)*... There obviously weren't any... 'cos I didn't take none home.

Jo was always like the top ten in her class, really good, going to hockey matches and things. She'd come in from school, go into the dining room and spend hours on her homework, and me and Johnnie'd be out every night. She was really brainy. We didn't care for or like each other. She thought I was a...

(JO enters.)

JO & JUDY: Scruffy horrible little idiot.

JUDY: She always put me down for...

JO & JUDY: ...wearing jeans, being scruffy and not bothering to look good.

JUDY: I remember one time when we were all talking about what we were going to wear to a wedding reception

JO: And what are you going to wear? Jeans?

JUDY: Yeh, probably will!

JO: How can you wear jeans to a wedding?

JUDY: I don't give a toss! If they don't like it they can sling me out! I'll wear what I want to wear!

*(Silence. **PETE** enters and presents **JUDY** with a "baby"… don't use a doll, a folded sheet is much more flexible and can be reused in a different way in the following scene.)*

JUDY: I got married when I was seventeen. Joanna was always out and about every night while I was the old frumpish housewife. When I split up with the man I was married to… (**PETE** *exits leaving* **JUDY** *with the "baby".*) I started going round with Jo 'cos she was working in Epping… but I still couldn't go out a lot 'cos I had my baby… Leanne.

*(**JUDY** puts the "baby" down… to sleep. **JO** enters… in a cameo scene they have "fun" punctuated by downing drink.)*

VI: Joanna was an absolute brick to Judy during that time. She'd take her out and help her with Leanne. She was absolutely brilliant.

JUDY: Jo didn't have a boyfriend, so she used to come round and stay with me. We was always laughing… everything would just crack you up… you'd think everything was funny.
One night… we'd been to see the New Vaudeville Band… you know… (*singing*) 'Winchester Cathedral'… not that we thought they were cool, but Jo knew one of the blokes.
Anyway we got to the traffic lights near the Indian restaurant in Epping and pulled down this entrance… I don't remember why. Anyway, we got stuck in loads of mud so Jo got out and pushed the car.

JO: When I say rev it up… rev it up!

JUDY: She was giving it an almighty push and I revved it up. She came round to me, and tapped on my window, deadly serious, I'll never forget, and said…

JO: You fucking idiot!

JUDY: When I turned round, I saw she was completely pebble dashed in mud! She was really dressed up in this beautiful suede jacket. Well, we were just in hysterics for about ten minutes before we could get the car out.

(They both laugh… sharing the memory.)

JUDY: When most people go out, they have a few drinks, have a nice evening out. We used to go out… and go mental. Jo could out-drink any bloke... whereas me... I'd have three glasses of wine and I'd be in a terrible state!

(They both laugh loudly... followed by a sudden silence. Turning slowly to the audience.)

JUDY: We was always out drinking. That's all we ever did... go out and go wild.
I'll tell you something that is really weird. It was really strange.
We were in her new flat doing some decorating and she said:

JO: I think I'll make a will.

JUDY: Joanna! You think of the most funny things! What on earth do you want to make a will for?

JO: I just feel that I should. I mean, if anything happens to me now I've got the flat, there could be quite a bit of money involved... and I'd want your Leanne to have it.

JUDY: What? You can't be serious.

JO: Well, you don't know this... but Denise did my Tarot cards... twice... and I got the death one... both times.

JUDY: Joanna! You shouldn't mess around with things like that. I'd never go into Denise's house... let alone do that! it's like the Evil Dead house... really creepy!

JO: Don't be stupid! What can happen to you?

JUDY: If I pulled it out, that'd be it! I'd be so frightened. I'd be like the Doomsday book, walking around, wondering when it's going to happen.

JO: You're being silly! Denise told me it doesn't necessarily mean that you, personally are going to die; it could mean the death of a relationship.

JUDY: Aren't you scared?

JO: No. Why? Should I be? *(Silence.)*

JUDY: One week later we had the accident. *(Silence.)*

The Monday before the accident I gets this phone call from Jo. *(Yawning.)* It was about five or six o'clock in the morning...

JO: It's me.

JUDY: What the hell do you want?

JO: Can you come and pick me up?

JUDY: Where are you?

JO: Saffron Walden police station.

JUDY: What've you done?

JO: Got stopped for drinking and driving and they won't let me drive my car home 'cos I'm still over the limit and I've got to get to work.

JUDY: Okay. I'll come and get you. Stay where you are. I went over there, took her to work and took her back to get her car in the evening. She didn't seem too bothered about it really.

What on earth are you going to do? How are you going to get to work if you're banned?

JO: I dunno. I'll have to think of a way round it when I've been to court.

JUDY: Well, there's not a lot of transport from Dunmow to Epping, is there?

JO: Don't worry! Alison goes into Epping at about the same time, she'll give me a lift. I'll get round it somehow... it's not your problem so don't worry!

JUDY: How much had you had to drink?

JO: Just the usual.

JUDY: Yeh?

JO: ...some wine... not a lot.

JUDY: Don't you see! You'll be banned! I bet you were well over the limit!

JO: Judy! You're more worried about it than I am! Look! I don't want anyone else to know. I want you to promise me you won't tell Mum. (*Pause.*) You know what she's like; it'll make her worry and it's not necessary.

JUDY: Okay then.

JO: I want you to promise.

JUDY: I won't tell Mum... I promise.

(*They freeze. Silence.*)

VI: The day of the accident Joanna phoned me and said...

JO: Are you coming into lunch today, Mum? Terry and Trisha are coming... so why don't you come too?

VI: So I did. We had a right old laugh, as you can imagine. Then we went back to her office, so that she could do some work and, like we was all in a laughing mood.
I left there about a quarter past five and she said she was meeting Judy

JO: She's coming to aerobics... I said if she came I'd take her to the wine bar after.

VI: Well, be careful in the car. If you're drinking, it may be best for you to stay at Judy's. It'd be stupid to travel all the way back to Dunmow.

JO: Mum!

VI: Just be careful!

JO: Mum! You worry when I go to the lav!

VI: "Yeh! I do!" *(Silence.)*

They were the last words I said to her.

Then I went home. *(They embrace.* **VI** *exits.)*

Section 3

THE ACCIDENT

JUDY: We'd been to the Epping Sports Centre doing an aerobics class, and after a couple of drinks there we went on to the wine bar. It was only around the corner so we walked. I wasn't drinking as much as Jo; I hadn't had an enormous amount; I should imagine about three quarters of a bottle of wine which to me isn't a lot of drink. I certainly didn't **feel** drunk. Jo had drunk an awful lot, so I suggested that it would be better if I drove:

JO: No! It's my car. It's my responsibility.

JUDY: Jo, what's going to happen if you do get pulled up? You'll go to court with two drink drive convictions which means a huge ban and a ridiculous fine!

JO: No, it's my car!

JUDY: Look, I haven't had as much to drink as you, so I'm only going to be a bit over the limit and anyway, even if I did get caught, it makes no odds 'cos I don't need to drive as much as you what with your job and...

JO: Okay then. You drive

*(**JO** throws the car keys to **JUDY**. They freeze the moment as **JUDY** catches the keys. Silence.)*

JUDY: We got into the car with me in the driving seat and put a tape on.

('We've Only Just Begun[1] by the Carpenters fades in slowly and underpins the duration of the accident scene.)

JUDY: It's only about five miles from the Epping Sports Centre to North Weald where I live. The last thing I remember is driving past the hospital.

P.C. CATEN: I was out with a fairly young PC. We'd been static at Scratch Bridge in North Weald for about half an hour.

---

[1] The performing rights for this play do not cover the right to use this or other pieces of pre-recorded music. Permission will be required from the appropriate bodies.

P.C. ABRAHAMS: As far as I can remember, it was about five to twelve and we'd decided to go in at midnight to have a cup of tea.

P.C. CATEN: As we made our way towards Epping, I happened to note Jo and Judy drive by. I'd known their family for… well over ten years. I supposed they'd been out enjoying themselves.

JUDY: I was used to driving a bigger car with powered steering and I guess what must have happened is that where I was a bit drunk I forgot I was in Jo's car and just didn't turn the wheel enough on this bend at Scratch Bridge. I can't remember going off the road, I can't remember hitting the kerb or anything. God, it must have took off when we hit that kerb. Every now and then I get flashbacks, I keep thinking that she told me to slow down, but I can't remember her being in the car. I can't really remember anything.

(The following speeches are made simultaneously.)

ACTOR 1: Okay then; you drive.

ACTOR 2: No it's my car it's my responsibility.

ACTOR 1: I think I'll make a will.

ACTOR 2: I'm only going to be a bit over the limit.

ACTOR 1: Them two. They're always pissed they'll be alright.

ACTOR 2: I got the death card both times.

ACTOR 1: Today's easy to follow recipe "Smashed out of our Skulls".

ACTOR 1&2: Okay then. You drive.

JUDY: Wouldn't it be better if I drove? What's going to happen if you do get pulled up? You'll go to court with two drink drive convictions which means a huge ban and a ridiculous fine!

I haven't had as much to drink as you, so I'm only going to be a bit over the limit and anyway, even if I did get caught, it makes no odds. I don't need to drive as much as you what with your job and…

JO: Judy! Slow down a bit!

The accident is simulated stylistically somehow!!! It has been presented in a variety of ways. I would suggest the use of scaffolding bars and loud screams… attempting to capture the essence of the accident… speed… impact… fright… whiplash… the sound of metal on metal… and finally silence and stillness.

Section 4

THE AFTERMATH

DUNCAN: I guess it was about midnight and there was one hell of a mighty crash, completely and utterly unannounced by any of the normal sounds that one might associate with a road accident... howls of tyres, screeching and what have you. I was just mesmerised. I couldn't think what it was and all I could hear was 'We've Only Just Begun' by The Carpenters blasting out from what I later discovered to be the car stereo. I got out of bed and looked out of the window.

SLIDE 1²

DUNCAN: There was a Renault 5 buried in the bridge, just literally sort of disappeared into the bridge parapet. My immediate reaction was "Oh shit! I don't want to be involved in that! I'll let someone else go and have a look." I waited... maybe half a minute, hoping that someone would get out of the bloody thing... but nobody did. In the end, I pulled on a pair of trousers, a pullover but stupidly nothing else and shot across there.

I couldn't approach the car from the passenger side it was too badly damaged so went to the driver's door. It wouldn't open. I looked inside. I could see two shapes. I tried the door again. The music was blasting out, like it was sort of force ten on the decibel scale.

At that point I suddenly realised that I was standing around in bare feet with a lot of glass about the place which was pretty bloody stupid. I thought... "Well, nobody else is coming out to help!", so I shot back inside, dialled 999, reported the accident... oh yes... and put some shoes on!

P.C. ABRAHAMS: We'd only gone about half a mile further, towards the police station, when our information room called up.

VOICE: *(FX over radio.)* Any unit to attend a serious RTA in North Weald.

---

² Slides, police photos of the accident to be shown in this scene are available from Salamander Street (info@salamanderstreet.com). They should be requested on confirmation of the licensing of performing rights.

SLIDE 2

P.C. ABRAHAMS: We can attend. We're in North Weald. Can you give us an exact location?

VOICE: *(FX over radio.)* The informant is telephoning from Harrison Drive. The accident was on Scratch Bridge.

P.C. ABRAHAMS: We'll attend. E.T.A. one minute.

DUNCAN: I went back to the car which was now smelling of petrol, battery fluid, anti freeze and there was this dripping and hissing. I was afraid it might catch fire so, put my leg up onto the back wing and forced the driver's side door open.

The music was still blasting out, so the first thing I did was to turn off the power which produced dead silence.

I was then confronted with these two forms and a strong smell of alcohol. I remember that clearly, the smell of alcohol and... well, cheap perfume. I felt for a pulse on the passenger. I couldn't find one. There were no... no life signs at all. *(Pause.)*

SLIDE 3

DUNCAN: The bridge they'd hit was just these upright concrete pillars with scaffolding pipes coming through them. One of these pipes had been bent, come straight in, through the windscreen, missed the driver... but it was such that the passenger had to have been hit by it. Her head was in a position where it had obviously been thrown back by the force of this pole coming in directly on... to her face. I was sufficiently squeamish not to investigate that one any further. Thank Christ it wasn't bloody daylight, that's all I can say.

I remember thinking... "the passenger is either dead or alive. If she's dead, well I can't do anything about it, but what if she starts to wake up, with hideous bloody injuries requiring some attention, what the bloody hell am I to do then?" I've done my bit of first aid, but this was way, way, way beyond that... or anything I'd experienced in my life.

That's the frightening thing about it. The fact that she was dead... was a bloody blessing!

(He goes to JUDY.)

By this time the driver had begun to make signs of recovery, so I managed to find the buckles of her seat belt and release her.

Right, let's get you out of here.

She was like a sort of bendy toy really... I soon realised that she was smashed out of her skull... drunk.

JUDY: What on earth happened down there?

DUNCAN: I'm afraid you've had a bit of an accident, dear. Can you tell me what your name is?

JUDY: Judy. *(Pause.)*

There was glass in the car. I remember glass and blood on the floor of the car; where did it all come from?

DUNCAN: We'll find out later.

JUDY: Where's my handbag? I want my handbag! It must be in the car!

DUNCAN: No, you hang on here a minute, love.

JUDY: My sister! I've got to get to Joanna! She's still in the car! Don't you bloody touch me! I want to go and see if she's alright!

DUNCAN: No! We'd better wait here. I've phoned the police, so they'll be here in a minute.

JUDY: What's wrong with Joanna? Fucking let go of me!

(She crumples. Resigned.)

Why won't you let me go back to the car?

DUNCAN: I thought she was going to get so hysterical that I just wouldn't be able to cope, but she didn't actually; she just seemed to go limpish and start to cry.

At that point the police car came down the road like a bat out of hell! I don't think that it had stopped before the doors were opened and a young PC ran out towards us.

There's someone else in the car.

P.C. ABRAHAMS: I'll go down.

DUNCAN: He went down to the passenger side of the vehicle and shone a torch in there. Obviously he was having difficulty seeing inside because he kept angling his head.

P.C. CATEN: It's Jo Poulton. I can't believe it! Jo and Judy.

P.C. ABRAHAMS: Do you know them then?

P.C. CATEN: Yeh. I can't get a pulse at all!

P.C. ABRAHAMS: Look! Smoke under the bonnet.

P.C. CATEN: You go and get the extinguisher... I'll phone HQ and then go and see the driver... she's Jo's sister. *(ABRAHAMS exits.* **P.C. CATEN** *speaking to radio.)* Golf-golf-two-one. Regarding RTA that we are attending in North Weald. We require immediate back up. Possible fatal. Will require two ambulances. I repeat **two** ambulances.

DUNCAN: I can remember holding this woman, listening to him report back and nodding as he said "fatal". She didn't hear anything. I'm absolutely positive that she had no idea at all... though she must have surely suspected something.

P.C. CATEN: Thanks for your help. It's good of you to come out.

DUNCAN: Is it okay for me to go back home now?

P.C. CATEN: Yeh. I know Judy... don't I, love... so I'll make sure that she's okay. Thanks again for coming out.

DUNCAN: I live over there. If you want any further information... feel free to knock.

I went back home and poured myself a great big bloody drink! I opened the curtains and stood and watched the proceedings... just out of morbid curiosity... I'm afraid that's inherent in all of us in those kinds of circumstances.

I remember feeling slightly angry that so many houses that faced onto it had obviously decided that they didn't want to become involved... it's just a silly sort of reaction you get in a state of stress... 'cos I do understand why... but bloody muggins here... why did I have to go out and get involved?

I didn't sleep at all. The realisation that you've come right next to an extremely violent death was a very unnerving and shattering experience... and it was annoying. This bloody woman who drove this bloody car hadn't even touched the brakes... well she couldn't have done! There wasn't a mark on the road anywhere! She was that drunk!

She didn't even know that she'd gone up the kerb, along the pavement and into the bridge parapet... she was that drunk!

P.C. CATEN: My main job now was to keep Judy away from the accident and her mind off Jo. She had glass in her hair, blood on her fingers, was very disorientated and continued to cry. I carried her to the police car and spoke to her to reassure her that everything that could be done was being done. Eventually the ambulance arrived.

Judy, where's your daughter? Where's Leanne?

JUDY: She's at home. I've got a baby-sitter. What'll happen?

P.C. CATEN: It's okay. I'll sort something out whilst you're being taken to hospital.

JUDY: What about Joanna? Isn't she coming?

P.C. CATEN: They're just getting her out. She'll be coming in another ambulance.

JUDY: Why can't she come in this one?

P.C. CATEN: I'm afraid that she's a bit more hurt than you are.

JUDY: Why can't we wait? I want her to come with me!

P.C. CATEN: No! We need another ambulance for her.

JUDY: I remember turning round as they put me in the ambulance and seeing the car hooked on the railings up in the air. I didn't see the front of the car at all. They kept me round my side of the car which was alright. It weren't smashed or nothing... it was all up in the air and like tipping forward and the wheels were off the ground and I thought... "Oh look at that!!" I didn't think that Jo had been really injured... it didn't even enter my mind that she could have been killed.

P.C. ABRAHAMS: After they'd got the passenger out of the car I had to keep members of the public who'd come out to watch away from the scene as it wasn't a particularly pretty sight. When they started to get her out of the car they realised that she had quite severe injuries so they had to... somebody got some black plastic bags which they put over her head and shoulders... just to make it a little bit better for people that were gathered around.

P.C. CATEN: We made our way to her mother's house. We had to break the news to her.

I will admit that I was controlling my feelings more than I've ever had to before.

I took a deep breath and knocked on the door.

P.C. ABRAHAMS: There was no reply. We tried several times again.

P.C. CATEN: That's strange. Judy said she'd be in.

P.C. ABRAHAMS: No one answered so we came away.

DUNCAN: *(As this speech is portrayed any "debris" from the accident can be cleared up.)*

I've recently been reading *The Shooting of President Kennedy*. He was apparently lying in the hospital after he died and the hospital was returning to normal. There was a comment made, that next door, two janitors... auxiliaries were laughing... laughing over a joke. There was this hollow laughter going down the corridor with a dead president there... a very harsh irony eh?

Well, a similar thing happened in this situation. The ambulance had gone, and you were left with the "roadies" trying to drag the car off the bridge parapet. They were laughing and I thought... that can't be right.

My final reaction was the following morning. I went out there and "society" had cleared up the mess. "Society" had come along with its back up force and cleaned up the mess... you know... the ambulance had taken away the broken body... and the mortuary had taken care of it from then on. There wasn't any blood... there wasn't anything. The place had been sanitised.

It was an extraordinary sensation, and yet a human life had disappeared there, and you felt... well I felt that there should be something there that actually proved the point... but there was nothing.

Section 5

BREAKING THE NEWS

VI: I woke up. I heard a rat-a-tat-tat at the door. I looked out of the window and saw a police car drive away and ... oh ... it's a sick feeling. Know what I mean? I thought ... something's happened to Johnnie ... he's been nicked or something ... so I came downstairs and rang Ongar police station. I couldn't get a reply so I rang Epping.

VOICE: Everything's alright, Mrs. Poulton. They were just trying to get in touch. I'll let them know you're there.

VI: I made a cup of coffee and sat down ... and ... oh your mind is going. They were very nice ... but... you know ... there's something inside you; you think: something's up. Ten minutes later they were back.

P.C. CATEN: Hello Vi.

VI: Chris! What is it? Is it Johnnie? It's Johnnie isn't it? *(Pause.)* Has something happened ... do you want to come in?

P.C. CATEN: Yes. Look I think you'd better sit down. I've got some very bad news for you.

VI: It's Johnnie ... I know what it's about. You know me ... I can take anything.

P.C. CATEN: Vi ... it's not to do with John at all.

(The following speeches are made simultaneously.)

VI: It's Jo. *(Silence.)* What's happened to her?	**JUDY:** *(Enters.)* Wouldn't it be better if I drove.
P.C. CATEN: Please sit down.	**JO:** *(Enters.)* No. It's my car. It's my responsibility.

JUDY: I haven't had as much to drink as you. I'll only be a bit over the limit.

JO: Judy! Slow down a bit!

*(**JUDY** screams and moves into a freeze reminiscent of the crash.)*

ACTORS 1 & 2, DUNCAN: Joanna, just be careful in the car. If you're drinking it may be best for you to stay at Judy's; it'd be stupid to travel all the way to Dunmow. Just be careful.

P.C. CATEN: Joanna's been killed in a road accident.

Fade up appropriate music prior to the commencement of the following speeches – made simultaneously. As the speeches begin, **JO** *and* **JUDY** *break out of their freeze and laugh hysterically, a dreamlike quotation from the scene where the car was stuck in the mud… a nightmarish memory of the happy sisters playing in* **VI**'s *mind. Throughout this hysterical laughter they look at* **VI**. *They stop laughing as they see* **VI** *become faint.*

P.C. CATEN:	**ACTOR 1:**	**DUNCAN:**
Vi. Listen.	Then we went back to	This bloody woman
She didn't suffer.	the office so she could	who drove this bloody
It was very quick.	do some work and…	car hadn't even
Vi… do you	like… we was all in	touched the brakes…
understand what I'm	a laughing mood. I	well she couldn't have
saying ?	left there at about	done! There wasn't
	a quarter past five	a mark on the road
(VI finds it difficult to take	and she said: "Judy's	anywhere! She was
in and becomes lost in her	coming to aerobics…	that drunk. She didn't
memories.)	I said if she came I'd	even know that she'd
	take her to the wine	gone up the kerb,
	bar after."	along the pavement
		and into the bridge
		parapet… she was
		that drunk!

(Song fades – all exit except **P.C. CATEN** *and* **VI**.

P.C. CATEN *gently comforts* **VI** *and encourages her to sit.)*

P.C. CATEN: She was a lovely girl. I've come here tonight because I thought it would help you to have someone you know breaking the news to you. You have got to pull yourself together and be very brave. Judy was involved as well. She's in hospital now, and she needs you.

VI: Does she know about Joanna?

P.C. CATEN: No they're waiting…

VI: Are you sure she's alright?

P.C. CATEN: She's in shock, but I don't think she has any serious injuries. They've taken her to St Margaret's Hospital.

(Silence.)

VI: Was it Jo's car?

P.C. CATEN: Yes... but... but Judy was driving.

VI: But Jo never let anyone drive her car...
Chris, are you sure?

P.C. CATEN: Yes, certain.

VI: But I don't understand... why would Judy be?... It doesn't make sense. Will I have to identify her?

P.C. CATEN: I've already done it.

VI: Do I have to see her?

P.C. CATEN: No. No you don't.

(Silence.)

VI: Do you think I ought to go to St Margaret's to see Judy?

P.C. CATEN: I think it's very important that you speak to her.

VI: No way did I want to know what had happened. I just wanted to remember Jo as she was when I walked out of the office. No way did I want to know. All I knew was that my Joanna was dead. Chris said that it was instantaneous.

It's strange, but, a few years before, I'd had a really nasty road accident, and I didn't remember a thing until I came round in the ambulance and then it was... oh, I hurt like hell. Well, Joanna never came round... and that's how I know she didn't suffer. So that experience has eased my mind about her last moments.

(VI cries/sobs. She is alone for some moments as appropriate pre-recorded music swells. P.C. CATEN leads VI out slowly. JO and JUDY enter from either side of the stage and direct their lines to the other. They build gradually to a climax... as though it is a row and perhaps again move into freeze motifs reminiscent of the accident.)

JO: It's my car. It's my responsibility.

JUDY: Jo, what's going to happen if you do get pulled up? You'll go to court with two drink drive convictions which means a huge ban and a ridiculous fine!

JO: No, it's my car!

JUDY: Look, I haven't had as much to drink as you, so I'm only going to be a bit over the limit and anyway, even if I did get caught, it makes no odds 'cos I don't need to drive as much as you what with your job and...

JO: Okay then. You drive. (*Exits.*) (*Silence.*)

Section 6

THE HOSPITAL

Enter **SISTER/CHARGE NURSE DAVIS** *with a wheelchair.* **JO** *exits.* **DAVIS** *gets* **JUDY** *to sit in the wheelchair.*

SISTER/CHARGE NURSE DAVIS: When the driver was brought in I was told that she had no obvious injuries, but was very shocked. The ambulance crew were absolutely shattered by the accident... it was horrific... they were devastated by the state of Judy's sister. I was told that she was being taken straight to the mortuary. We felt that it was in Judy's best interests to delay telling her about her sister until she had some family support. I went over to her to take her through to casualty.

JUDY: *(Referring to the wheelchair.)* I don't need this! I ain't a bleedin' cripple!

DAVIS: You can't walk on your own just yet.

JUDY: Well, I don't want this fucking blanket.

DAVIS: You'll have to. You're in shock and you might catch a chill.

She was shaking, crying, a bit hysterical, typical road accident, very fraught ... very upset.

JUDY: Where's my sister? She is alright isn't she? Come on ... where is she?

DAVIS: Well, we're not quite sure. We're doing our best to get in contact with your mum. Now you're going to have to put on a hospital gown. The doctor wants to examine you to see if you're injured at all. I'll leave you here for a moment so that you can get changed.

You do sometimes feel aggressive to drunk drivers. I thought... you silly girl ... how could you have done this? Didn't you realise what could happen? You deliberately chose to drive. She just didn't consider that she could end up killing somebody... killing her own sister.

JUDY: I want to see Joanna. That's all I want to do. Why won't you let me?

DAVIS: You'll have to see the traffic police first. They should be here in a minute.

JUDY: What are they going to do?

DAVIS: Well, you know, if they do charge you, you'll have to face up to it, but then again, it's not the end of the world. People do get done for bad driving; they pay their fine and that's the end of it.

Fortunately, that night casualty wasn't that busy so I was able to sit with her for a considerable time... it seemed like a lifetime actually. I talked to her about her baby. I'd just become a granny. I was using delaying tactics, to stop her from getting too close to the fact that her sister had actually been killed. I didn't want to give her the chance to ask me what was happening. I think she probably knew, but just didn't dare ask. She didn't want to hear the answer. Yes, she must have realised we were stalling.

JUDY: I was ever so confused. It was like... like being in a ball of cotton wool and trying to get out and make sense of everything and I couldn't.

The main thing I wanted to know was that Joanna was okay. I was, so, I thought she'd only have a couple of scratches. I mean... it was only a short journey and from where I was stood, the car didn't look too bad. There were no other cars involved. I just didn't think it could have been that serious.

DAVIS: It looks as though the traffic police have arrived. They'll want to breathalyse you.

JUDY: So long as you'll let me see my sister!

DAVIS: They breathalysed her. It was positive. 184 milligrams. Over two times the legal limit.

JUDY: Right! Now can I see Jo?

DAVIS: I'll let you go in a minute... I promise you.

JUDY: You knew I wanted to see her! That's why I co-operated! I'm getting out of this stupid bloody thing to look for her on my own.

DAVIS: *(Restraining* **JUDY.***)* You have to stay here! We can't have patients walking around the hospital. I'm sorry but you'll have to wait.

JUDY: She must have thought I was a maniac!

I remember being stuck in this poxy hospital when I really wanted to go home. I hated it there. I hate hospitals anyway. I hate being ill and they all seemed to think something was wrong with me.

I didn't have any aches or pains or nothing... well... some cuts on my knuckles... little diddy cuts where all the glass had smashed in... but, I saw no reason to stay there!

DAVIS: I remember Mum arriving. It was very tense... very fraught.

P.C. CATEN: *(To* **VI.***)* This is Sister *(or, Charge Nurse)* Davis.

DAVIS: I've been looking after Judy.

P.C. CATEN: Perhaps it would be a good idea for you to go and have a cup of tea with Sister *(or, Charge Nurse)* Davis while I explain the whole situation to Judy.

DAVIS: Would you like to come this way, Mrs. Poulton?

P.C. CATEN: Judy. **(JUDY** *turns the wheelchair to face him.)*

JUDY: Please, Chris... please tell me what's going on... why are they keeping me here?

P.C. CATEN: I want you to be really brave.

JUDY: Why? What's wrong? What are they going to do to me?

P.C. CATEN: Promise me you're going to be really brave.

JUDY: Just tell me what's wrong!

P.C. CATEN: Judy... Joanna died in the accident.

(Silence.)

JUDY: You're lying. What a horrible thing to say! How can anybody say that to someone?

P.C. CATEN: I'm really, really sorry. I know it's a horrible thing to say but it is true. Jo did die in the accident.

JUDY: I don't believe it! You must be lying! I'm not hurt... so why is Jo?

P.C. CATEN: Judy... I'm not lying to you. You know me better than that.

JUDY: I don't believe you. Let me see her... then I'll believe you.

P.C. CATEN: No... you won't want to see her.

JUDY: Why? Was it really horrible? *(Silence.)*
Just tell me what's happened to her.

P.C. CATEN: It doesn't matter now, Judy.

JUDY: No. Not my sister... *(Breaking down.)* not my beautiful sister. Why the hell did I do it? (Pause.) What will Mum say?

P.C. CATEN: I've already seen your mum.

JUDY: What did she say? Is she here? I don't want to see her... I can't!

P.C. CATEN: She's not blaming you. She's very concerned about you.

JUDY: You've told her about Jo?

P.C. CATEN: Yes. *(Pause.)*
She's obviously very upset and she's going to need your support very much.

JUDY: Where is she?

P.C. CATEN: She's with Sister *(or, Charge Nurse)* Davis... having a cup of tea.

JUDY: She's here!

P.C. CATEN: Yes.

JUDY: No!

P.C. CATEN: Now listen... listen to me carefully. *(Pause.)* Your mum is not blaming you for the accident. She's not going to come in here and have a go at you. She is very concerned about you. Do you understand what I'm saying, Judy?

JUDY: Yes.

P.C. CATEN: You've both lost someone very close to you... and you're both very upset.

DAVIS: I was a bit apprehensive about how Mum would react. I half wondered if she might go in there and belt the life out of Judy. I was thinking how I would react in the same situation... I could identify with her in that I'd got two daughters about the same age. I was quite fraught about the whole thing.

P.C. CATEN: Judy's ready to see you, Vi. Now, don't forget what I said... you're going to have to put on a brave face regardless of how much it hurts, otherwise Judy's going to blame herself for Jo's death. It's

34

clearly very important that she doesn't do that. Sister *(or Charge Nurse)* Davis will show you the way. Vi... go and comfort her.

DAVIS: Are you going to be okay?

VI: Yes... don't worry. *(Silence.)*

There were curtains in front of each cubicle. Judy was in the fourth cubicle. She was sitting in a wheelchair. She was obviously shocked. She was I suppose... like a zombie ... just couldn't relate to anything. She was... like... white as a sheet and just kept looking ... staring at me. I felt she was waiting for me to have a go at her ... which was the last thing in the world I was going to do.

(They embrace.)

JUDY: I just can't stand it. I'll never be able to live again!

VI: Come on, kid. We'll get you home.

JUDY: Mum. I wouldn't have driven if it hadn't been ... I'm not supposed to tell you ... but she ... I only drove because Jo'd already been convicted. I wasn't meant to tell you ... she made me promise not to tell you. She didn't want you to worry. I'm really, really sorry Mum!

VI: It was an accident. Come on. Chris has got his car. He's going to get us home.

JUDY: There was an instant of panic when I had to get into the car. I sort of backed off and thought "Oh no!", but I just sort of got into the car.

VI: When we got home I sat her down by the fire ... just Judy and me ... and I said: No way in the world do I blame you. I love you very, very much. I need you as much as you need me. I desperately need you to help me. You've got to help me, Judy. I'll help you but you've got to help your mum, Judy. I'll help you ... but you've got to help me through this too."

Then, we just drifted into talking about ordinary things.

Section 7

IN RETROSPECT

JUDY: I remember thinking that the next morning it would turn out to have been a nightmare. I'd be at home in my bed and I'd think... "What a horrible nightmare that was." But it wasn't... obviously... I was just in a kind of daze.

I kept thinking the phone was going to ring and it's going to be Joanna, and she's going to say "Ha ha this was a joke" – and I'd think "Oh what a sick joke!" ...

I used to think that there'd be a knock at the door and things like that. You think of anything except facing the truth of what's happened. I thought that for about six months.

I just couldn't accept it.

I had a nightmare not long ago about it. All I can remember is that I turned round and saw Joanna sitting in the car... really horrible... munched up and she turned to me and said...

"Look what you've done to my face!"

That really freaked me out, because, for the first time, it made me wonder... would she have forgiven me if she had survived? Well, would you?

Needless to say, I didn't sleep at all for the rest of that night. When I got my clothes back they were, like... smothered in big globs of blood. It was horrible... I wasn't expecting it and I had to have it cleaned.

Do you know... I hadn't talked to anyone about the accident before Mark... like, Mark Wheeller interviewed me for this play, three years after it happened. Chris Caten had said it might do some good... so that's why I did it. Without this I'd've probably never talked about it. I still think about it every day. It may just be a one second thought through my mind... like...

"Why did I ever do that?", but I did... didn't I?

And that's all there is to it.

If I had one wish in the whole world, it'd be to go back to that night and...

JUDY & JO: Two sisters from Essex... out on the town.

JO: Losing weight...

JUDY: Till half past eight...

JO & JUDY: Then... off to the wine bar!

JUDY: *(Adopting the voice of typical cookery TV personality.)* Today's new easy to follow recipe is "Smashed out of our Skulls" by Judy...

JO: ... and Jo

JO & JUDY: Ingredients.

JO: Puerile conversation.

JUDY: Wine.

JO: Laughter.

JUDY: More wine!

JO: Visit the loo.

JUDY: And finally...

ALL: More wine!

JUDY: Note:

JO: This recipe can be improved with a healthy portion of...

JO & JUDY: Testosterone!

JO, JUDY, BOB & NOB: Cue... Blokes in the wine bar!

BOB: Bob...

NOB: Nob!

BOB: Looking good...

NOB: ... with slicked back hair.

BOB: Feeling cool...

BOB & NOB: No underwear!

BOB: With throbbing – can't get enough of it – body tone.

NOB: That's why they call us...

BOB & NOB: "Testosterone"

BOB: We are on the look out!

NOB: Fishing line and hook out!

BOB: Watering the nookey drought!

BOB & NOB: Essex girls!!!

JO & JUDY: Like two warriors they approach us...

JO: ... that one's mine!

JUDY: "Good luck to you", I reply, as they trot out...

JO & JUDY: ... their crappy chat up line.

BOB: Look at you two...

BOB & NOB: ... with your curves...

NOB: ... and us...

BOB & NOB: ... us with no brakes.

JO: Judy. What do you think?

JUDY: I think they're...

JO & JUDY: ... plonkers! *(They laugh hysterically.)*

BOB & NOB: Do you wanna drink?

JUDY & JO: *(Dead serious.)* Dry white wine... a bottle... each!

ALL 4: Drink!

BOB: Drink!

JUDY: Drink!

NOB: Drink!

JO: Drink!

> *(General merriment... perhaps a rowdy [rugby?] song.)*

JO: A bottle of wine and I'm still standing! (Laughter.) Come on Judy, we'd better get out before we're thrown out.

JUDY: You're not going to drive home in that state are you, Jo?

JO: I'm alright... don't worry about me!

JUDY: Why don't we catch a cab? It'll only be a couple of quid. I'll bring you back here to pick the car up tomorrow afternoon.

JO: You're like our mum you are... worry, worry, worry.

JUDY: Come on, Jo... I'll pay.

JO: Oh alright then... anything to keep you quiet.

JUDY: You go and phone... I'll go and get your stuff from the car... can I have the keys? *(*JO *throws the keys to* JUDY. *She catches them.* JO *exits.* JUDY *is alone on stage. Slowly she turns to the audience.)*

But I can't ever go back to that night... I realise that... so, resigned. I think that's the word. I'm resigned to the fact that it's happened. There's no way that I'm suddenly a pure white character with no faults. It hasn't put me off drink. I still have a glass of wine, or half a lager... but I will never drink and drive again as long as I live... never ever. I just couldn't do it.

JUDY'S MONOLOGUE

Please feel free to edit sensitively where necessary.

JUDY: The accident happened on the 20th May 1983. Resigned... I think that's the word. I'm resigned to the fact that it has happened.

If you go through life with a big guilt complex afterwards, you just end up hurting everybody else as well as yourself, 'cos you get bitter and wound up. Nothing I can do is going to change it, ever. I wouldn't have harmed Joanna, my sister, not on purpose, so I don't feel guilty about killing her... because it was... an accident.

You get so sure of yourself, so clever, well, not clever... you just don't think, 'cos you do it all the time. It only takes one person to point it out to you and you might not do it.

Before it happens you think... "Oh, I won't get caught!" I would probably never have got stopped and breathalysed. I'm having to pay for my mistake in a different way.

I still think about it every day. It may just be a one second thought through my mind... like... "Why did I ever do that?", but I did... didn't I? And that's all there is to it.

At first, I kept thinking the phone was going to ring and it's going to be Joanna, and she's going to say "Ha ha this was a joke", – and I'd think... "Oh what a sick joke!"

I used to think that there'd be a knock at the door and things like that. You think of anything except facing the truth of what's happened. I thought that for about six months. I just couldn't accept it.

I remember thinking that the next morning it would turn out to have been a nightmare. I'd be at home in my bed and I'd think... "What a horrible nightmare that was." But it wasn't... obviously... I was just in a kind of daze.

I actually did have a nightmare not long ago about it. All I can remember is that I turned round and saw Joanna sitting in the car... really horrible... munched up and she turned to me and said... "Look what you've done to my face!" That really freaked me out, because for the first time it made me wonder... would she have forgiven me if she had survived?

Well, would you?

40

Needless to say, I didn't sleep at all for the rest of that night. When I got my clothes back they were, like... smothered in big globs of blood... it was horrible... I wasn't expecting it. I had to have it cleaned.

I hadn't talked to anyone about the accident before Mark, like Mark Wheeller interviewed me for this play, three years after Jo's death. Chris Caten said it might do some good, so that's why I did it. Without this I'd've probably never talked about it.

If I had one wish in the whole world, it'd be to go back to that night and... but I can't... I realise that so, resigned... I think that's the word. I'm resigned to the fact that it's happened.

There's no way that I'm suddenly a pure white character with no faults. It hasn't put me off drink. I still have a glass of wine, or half a lager... but I will never drink and drive again as long as I live... never ever... I just couldn't do it.

Digital Resources for Teachers

There are a number of practical digital resources for teachers and students who are studying *Too Much Punch for Judy* as a set text.

The Story Behind... ... Too Much Punch for Judy by Mark Wheeller is available from Salamander Street.

A video recording is also available for download – please see the *Too Much Punch for Judy* page on www.salamanderstreet.com for further details.

Too Much Punch For Judy DVD/Download

By Oasis Youth Theatre, directed by Mark Wheeller (assisted by Charlie Wheeller – Barely Methodical Circus Troupe – choreography of the crash scene which has proved inspirational for students around the world).

"This play remains as powerful and relevant as ever. It packed a thoroughly knock out punch. I absolutely loved the performance... loved it! The physicality throughout was excellent! Oasis Youth Theatre are as committed and disciplined group of young people as you will ever see." Paul Fowler GODA adjudicator (Quarter Final of All England Theatre Festival)

This is the DVD of the unabridged production and includes bonus features:

Interview with Mark Wheeller, original cast members from 1987 and Ape Theatre Company Director Matt Allen. *Too Much Punch For Judy* has toured across the UK since 1989 and continues to be toured annually in Jersey. It has had 6049 licensed performances (June 2019) and still counting.

In light of this recent announcement from BTEC this DVD/download will provide opportunities to study Wheellerplays:

'You'll be pleased to hear that we will allow Mark Wheeller's plays to be used in Component 1 of the Tech Award. If it has recordings of a professional, student or youth theatre production that you can access, you are free to select it for use in Component 1.' **PAUL WEBSTER**

Available from Salamander Street.

The Story Behind... Too Much Punch for Judy

By Mark Wheeller

"This book was enthralling from start to finish. Not only does it give a clear insight into how Too Much Punch for Judy evolved, it reminds you of the energy and integrity true drama can bring. Without exaggerating Mark Wheeller's page turner inspired me to give up my leadership duties and get back into the drama studio with my amazing students. Even if you do not discover your Road to Damascus moment you'll be a lot clearer about Too Much Punch for Judy!!"

Andy – Amazon review from the first edition of the book.

Too Much Punch For Judy is one of, (or perhaps even) the most performed contemporary play(s). Performed 6,058 times to June 2020. Messages from students studying the play, asking Mark Wheeller about its background, sparked the idea for this unique book.

Barrie Sapsford, who played Chris Caten in the original Epping Youth Theatre production, worked with Mark to design this attractive and accessible book.

* Social and historical information on how and why the play came to be developed, including original diary extracts from Mark Wheeller

* Ideas on how to stage the seemingly impossible accident scene

* Improvisation ideas used with the original cast to enhance performances

*The story of Judy (the person and the play) during, and after the play

"I thoroughly recommend this to other teachers, students, practitioners. It is fantastic to see a resource that will benefit both teacher and student in staging this play. As with 'Drama Schemes,' the book is well laid out, an engaging and insightful read."

Olivia Murphy, Drama and Performing Arts teacher, Bitterne Park School, Hampshire

Paperback 9781913630379
eBook 9781913630386

Available from Salamander Street and all good bookshops.

Teachers – if you are interested in buying a set of texts
for your class please email info@salamanderstreet.com
– we would be happy to discuss discounts and keep you up to
date with our latest publications and study guides.

Pandemexplosion
Paperback 9781914228841

Mark Wheeller's Silas Marner
Paperback 9781913630805
eBook 9781913630799

Missing Dan Nolan
Paperback 9781913630287
eBook 9781913630294

Chicken!
Paperback 9781913630331
eBook 9781913630324

Chequered Flags to Chequered Futures
Paperback 9781913630355
eBook 9781913630348

Game Over
Paperback 9781913630263
eBook 9781913630270

Hard to Swallow
Paperback 9781913630249
eBook 9781913630256

Hard to Swallow, Easy to Digest
(with Karen Latto)
Paperback 9781913630409
eBook 9781913630393

Hard to Swallow, Easy to Digest: Student Workbook
Paperback 9781913630416
eBook 9781913630423

The Story Behind ... Too Much Punch for Judy
Paperback 9781913630379
eBook 9781913630386

Printed in the USA
CPSIA information can be obtained
at www.ICGtesting.com
JSHW080007150824
68134JS00021B/2334